African Animals

Elephants

ABDO
Publishing Company

Big
Buddy BOOKS
African Animals

by Julie Murray

VISIT US AT
www.abdopublishing.com

Published by ABDO Publishing Company, PO Box 398166, Minneapolis, MN 55439.

Printed in the United States of America, North Mankato, Minnesota.
102011
012012
♻ PRINTED ON RECYCLED PAPER

Coordinating Series Editor: Rochelle Baltzer
Editor: Marcia Zappa
Contributing Editors: Megan M. Gunderson, BreAnn Rumsch, Sarah Tieck
Graphic Design: Maria Hosley
Cover Photograph: *iStockphoto*: ©iStockphoto.com/namibelephant.
Interior Photographs/Illustrations: *Corbis* (pp. 8, 13); *iStockphoto*: ©iStockphoto.com/brytta (p. 4), ©iStockphoto.com/PTB-images (p. 4), ©iStockphoto.com/Taalvi (p. 12); *Minden Pictures*: Ian Redmond/npl (p. 7); *Photolibrary*: Age fotostock (p. 21), Bios (pp. 7, 17, 19, 27), Bridge (p. 21), First Light Associated Photographers (p. 17), Imagebroker.net/Heiner Heine (p. 9), Oxford Scientific (OSF) (pp. 9, 23, 25); *Shutterstock*: Paul Banton (p. 5), Four Oaks (pp. 27, 29), Eric Isselée (p. 12), javarman (p. 9), Villiers Steyn (p. 15), Gert Johannes Jacobus Vrey (p. 11), Dana Ward (p. 9), Warren Price Photography (p. 28).

Library of Congress Cataloging-in-Publication Data

Murray, Julie, 1969-
  Elephants / Julie Murray.
    p. cm. -- (African animals)
  ISBN 978-1-61783-218-5
  1. Elephants--Juvenile literature. I. Title.
  QL737.P98M8675 2012
  599.67--dc23
                      2011027844

Contents

Long ago, nearly all land on Earth was one big mass. About 200 million years ago, the land began to break into **continents**. One of these is called Africa.

African elephants are the heaviest land animals in the world.

Africa is the second-largest **continent**. It is known for hot weather, wild land, and interesting animals. One of these animals is the African elephant. In the wild, these elephants are only found in Africa.

Elephant Territory

There are two types of African elephants. These are savanna elephants and forest elephants.

Savanna elephants live south of the Sahara Desert. They are most common in dry grasslands and open woodlands.

Forest elephants are less well known. They live in western and central Africa. They are most often found in thick rain forests.

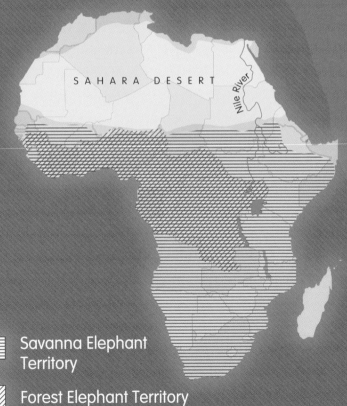

SAHARA DESERT

Nile River

 Savanna Elephant Territory

Forest Elephant Territory

Africa's rain forests are home to many uncommon animals. Forest elephants share them with gorillas and pygmy hippopotamuses.

Elephants are so strong, they can knock down whole trees! Then, they eat the leaves at the top. This helps keep grasslands open.

Jambo! Welcome to Africa!

If you took a trip to where elephants live, you might find…

TROPIC OF CAPRICORN

…many languages.

More than 1,000 languages are spoken across Africa! Swahili (swah-HEE-lee) is common in eastern and central Africa where many elephants live. In Swahili, *jambo* is a greeting for visitors. *Masalala* means "goodness!" or "wow!" And *tembo* means "elephant."

…a big daily meal.

In African villages, most people eat only one large meal each day. In the evening, they gather to eat with family and friends. The rest of the day, they eat snacks.

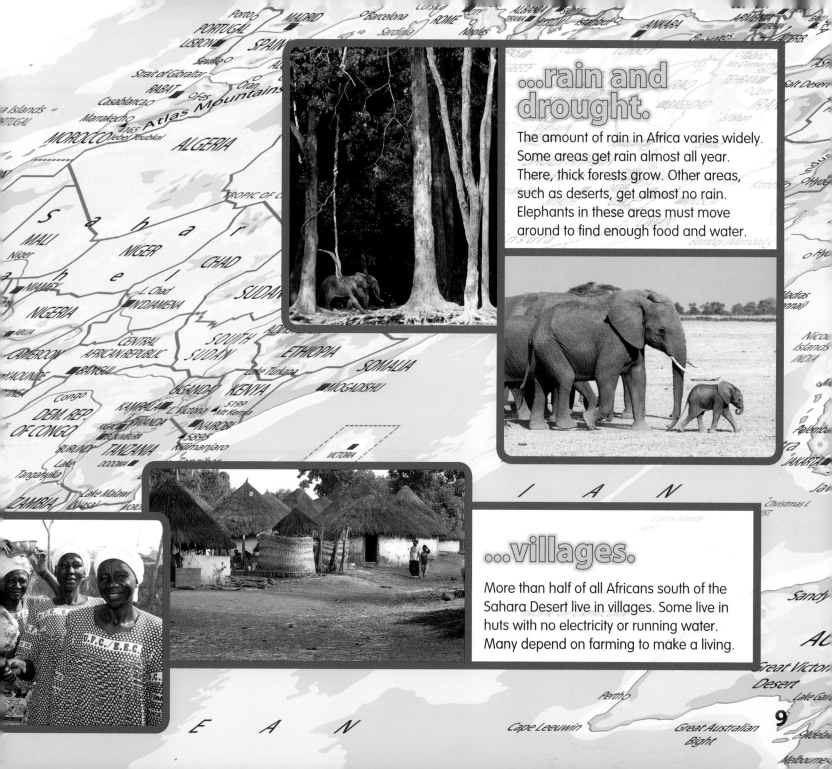

...rain and drought.

The amount of rain in Africa varies widely. Some areas get rain almost all year. There, thick forests grow. Other areas, such as deserts, get almost no rain. Elephants in these areas must move around to find enough food and water.

...villages.

More than half of all Africans south of the Sahara Desert live in villages. Some live in huts with no electricity or running water. Many depend on farming to make a living.

Take a Closer Look

Elephants are huge animals! Males are usually larger than females. Adult male savanna elephants weigh about 12,000 pounds (5,400 kg). They can be 11 feet (3.4 m) tall.

Forest elephants are smaller. Adult males weigh up to 10,000 pounds (4,500 kg). They are usually 8 feet (2.4 m) tall or less.

Uncovered!
Adult elephants are so large they have no natural predators. But sometimes, lions and other large animals hunt baby elephants.

An average car weighs about 4,000 pounds (1,800 kg). An adult male savanna elephant can weigh three times that much!

An African elephant has a round body and thick legs. Its large head has small eyes, big ears, and a long trunk. It also has long ivory teeth called tusks. An African elephant's body is covered in thick, gray skin with deep wrinkles.

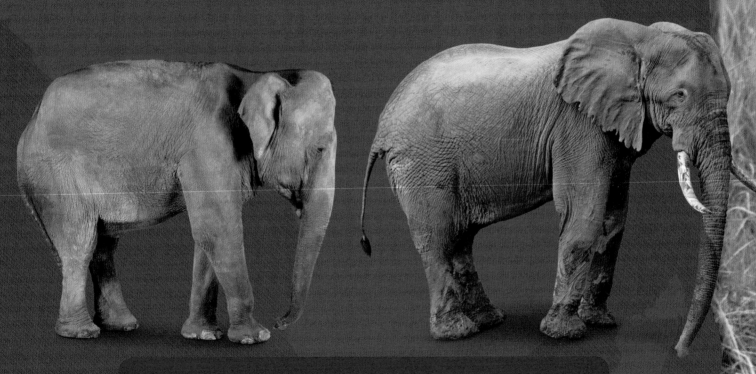

Asian elephants (*above left*) look different from African elephants (*above right*). They often weigh less. They have smaller ears and smoother skin. And their backs are rounded, while the backs of African elephants have a dip.

A savanna elephant's ears can be four feet (1.2 m) wide! Its ear shape looks like the continent of Africa.

Talented Trunks

Elephants are the only animals on Earth with trunks. An elephant's long trunk is actually its upper lip and nose! Elephants use their trunks for smelling and breathing. They also use them to drink water, grab objects, and make noises.

To drink, an elephant sucks water partway up its trunk. Then, it curls its trunk up and sprays the water into its mouth.

An adult savanna elephant's trunk is about seven feet (2 m) long. That is longer than most humans are tall! It has about 100,000 **muscles** but no bones.

At the end of an African elephant's trunk are two fingerlike parts. These can pick up small objects, such as berries or leaves.

A baby elephant often uses its trunk to hold on to its mother's tail. This helps them stay together.

Elephants use their long trunks to grab leaves from tall trees.

Keeping Cool

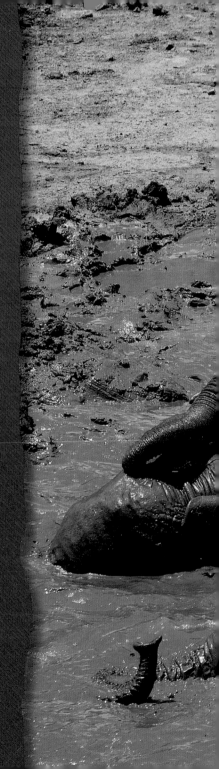

Most parts of Africa are hot year round. Elephants don't sweat. So, they have to keep cool in other ways.

One way elephants stay cool is by flapping their ears. This cools the blood inside their ears. Then, the cooled blood flows through their bodies.

Elephants also take showers to cool off! They suck water into their trunks and spray themselves. Then, they spray dust on their skin. This guards them from the sun.

Rolling in mud is another way elephants guard their skin from the hot sun.

Mealtime

African elephants are big eaters. An adult savanna elephant usually eats more than 300 pounds (140 kg) of food each day! They eat grasses, roots, leaves, fruit, and bark.

African elephants drink more than 40 gallons (150 L) of water each day. Often, they must walk far to find enough food and water.

African elephants spend about 16 hours each day eating.

Elephants use their tusks to dig up roots and tear bark off trees.

21

Herd Life

Elephants are **social** animals. Females and young elephants live together in herds. A herd is made up of four to ten adults from the same family and their young. A leader called a matriarch (MAY-tree-ahrk) guides each herd.

Male elephants leave the herd when they are 13 to 20 years old. They often live alone or in groups of their own. When they get older, male elephants visit herds to **mate**.

The matriarch is usually the oldest and largest female in the herd. She uses her good memory to guide her herd to food and water.

Elephants **communicate** with each other in many ways. They make sounds including rumbles, screams, groans, and squeaks. They use their trunks to make loud trumpeting noises when scared.

Elephants also use their trunks to play fight. And, they touch each other with their trunks as a greeting.

Uncovered!

Some elephant calls cannot be heard by people. Yet elephants can hear these low noises from several miles away!

Sometimes, elephants greet each other by wrapping their trunks together. This is similar to a hug.

25

Baby Elephants

Elephant calves can walk less than an hour after they are born. Soon, they can run and play too.

Elephants are **mammals**. Female elephants usually have one baby every two to five years. Baby elephants are called calves. At birth, they are already about three feet (1 m) tall. And, they often weigh more than 200 pounds (90 kg)!

At first, a calf drinks its mother's milk. After about three months, it starts to eat plants. All the female adults in a herd help take care of the calves.

Elephant calves are often covered in thin hair. It wears off as they grow.

Uncovered!
A baby elephant grows inside its mother for 22 months before it is born. That is longer than any other mammal!

Survivors

African elephants live 50 to 70 years in the wild!

African elephants face many dangers. New buildings and farms take over their **habitats**. Food and water can be hard to find during **droughts**. And, humans hunt elephants for their ivory tusks.

Still, elephants **survive**. Today, it is against the law to sell ivory to most countries. And, many people work to save elephant habitats. Elephants help make Africa an amazing place!

Many people consider ivory valuable. It is mostly used to make decorative objects such as carvings.

28

Uncovered!
African elephants are vulnerable. This means they are in danger of dying out.

Masalala!
I'll bet you never knew...

...that an elephant's skin is thick. In some areas, it is more than one inch (2.5 cm) thick! Still, an elephant can feel a small bug landing on it.

...that tusks are not an elephant's only teeth. They also have molars that help them smash food. One elephant molar can weigh as much as a brick!

...that the word *jumbo* comes from a famous elephant's name. In the 1800s, there was an African elephant named Jumbo. He lived in a zoo and later became part of a circus. Today, *jumbo* is used to describe anything really big.

...that elephants are good swimmers. In deep water, they breathe by holding their trunks above their heads.

Important Words

communicate (kuh-MYOO-nuh-kayt) to share knowledge, thoughts, or feelings.

continent one of Earth's seven main land areas.

drought (DRAUT) a long period of dry weather.

habitat a place where a living thing is naturally found.

mammal a member of a group of living beings. Mammals make milk to feed their babies and usually have hair or fur on their skin.

mate to join as a couple in order to reproduce, or have babies.

muscles (MUH-suhls) body tissues, or layers of cells, that help move the body.

social (SOH-shuhl) naturally living or growing in groups.

survive to continue to live or exist.

Web Sites

To learn more about elephants, visit ABDO Publishing Company online. Web sites about elephants are featured on our Book Links page. These links are routinely monitored and updated to provide the most current information available.

www.abdopublishing.com

31

Index